Cranbury
Public
Library

23 North Main St
(609)

WE CAN READ about NATURE!™

WHO DUG THIS HOLE?

by ANITA HOLMES

***B*ENCHMARK *B*OOKS**

MARSHALL CAVENDISH
NEW YORK

With thanks to
Susan Jefferson, first grade teacher at Miamitown
Elementary, Ohio, for sharing her innovative teaching
techniques in the Fun with Phonics section.

Benchmark Books
Marshall Cavendish Corporation
99 White Plains Road
Tarrytown, New York 10591

Text copyright © 2001 by Marshall Cavendish

All rights reserved. No part of this book may be reproduced in any form
without written permission from the publisher.

Photo Research by Candlepants, Inc.

Cover Photo: *Animal Animals* / Robert Lubeck

The photographs in this book are used by permission and through the courtesy of:
Corbis: Owen Franklin, 4-5. *Animals Animals:* Victoria McCormick, 6; Peter Weiman, 7;
Larry Crowhurst, 10; Robert Maier, 11; George Bernard, 19 (bottom); O.S.F., 20; Paton,
W./Survi OSF, 21; Don Enger, 23. *Photo Researchers, Inc.:* Rod Planck, 8,9; Helen
Williams, 12; Tom McHugh, 13; Bill Bachman, 14; George D. Lepp; John Dommers, 16;
Scott Camazine, 17; Stephen J. Krasemann, 18 (top); E.R. Degginger, 18 (bottom); Dr.
Paul A. Zahl, 19 (top); William H. Mullins, 22; Craig K. Lorenz, 24, 25; Nick Bergkessel,
27; Leonard Lee Rue III, 28.

Library of Congress Cataloging-in-Publication Data

Holmes, Anita, date
Who dug this hole? / by Anita Holmes.
p. cm.— (We can read about nature!)
Includes bibliographical references (p).
Summary: Describes animals that make homes in the ground, including the ghost
crab, chipmunk, and prairie dog.
ISBN 0-7614-1112-7
1. Burrowing animals—Habitations—Juvenile literature. [Burrowing animals. 2.
Animals—Habitations.] I. Title.
QL756.15.H66 2001   591.56'48—dc21   99-088055

Printed in Italy

1 3 5 6 4 2

Look for us inside this book.

ant
chipmunk
crab
mole
owl
prairie dog
rabbit
skunk
snake
spider
vole
wasp
wolf
woodpecker
worm

Have you ever dug a hole
in the sand?

It's cool and moist inside
and a good place to hide.

Look at this sandy beach.
It's full of little holes.

Who dug these holes?

Ghost crabs.
Here's a little digger now.

A ghost crab cleans out its hole.

Crabs use their large claws
to dig deep down.
They go inside to sleep
and to hide.

Who dug this hole?
A fiddler crab.

What a big claw!

Clams tunnel into the sand.
When the tide goes out,
the clams stay cool and damp.
When the tide comes in,
they move up to feed.

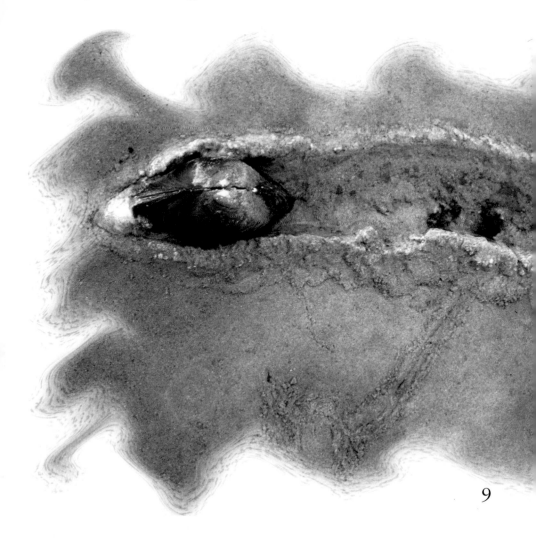

Some animals dig holes in the soil.
A mole's large paws are made
for digging.

Ooph! This hole is tight!

Moles are almost blind.
They live their whole lives underground.
Their homes are very dark, but cozy.

Prairie dogs build huge towns
underground.

Their homes have many rooms.
One pops up and looks around.

A black-tailed prairie dog and pups.

A black-tailed prairie dog and pups.

The pups are quick to follow.

Ants dig ant towns underground.

They live in groups called colonies. They work hard to build their towns and take care of each other.

An ant tries to move two larvae.

Some ants build towns in wood.

Carpenter ants and eggs in a log

Many wasps build homes in wood.
Others live in holes in the soil.

A yellow jacket nest

Lots of animals live in the ground . . .

a vole . . .

An arctic vole

a worm . . .

An earthworm

18

a spider . . .

A trap-door spider

a snake.

A racer snake

A rabbit moves along
its burrow in the soil.

It comes up to nibble grass
and have a drink of water.

Who dug this hole?
It's very big!

A mother wolf.
Her pup is safe inside.

A timber wolf with young

A Gila woodpecker in a saguaro

It's hot in the desert.
A woodpecker pecked a hole
in a giant cactus.
It's cool inside.

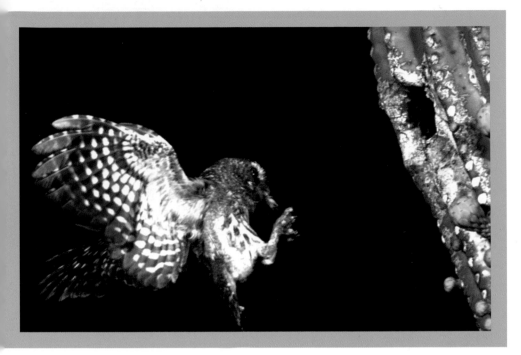

An elf owl

This owl found an empty hole.
Will it be safe there?

This chipmunk guards its home.
Its cheeks are full of nuts.
It stores the nuts underground
to eat in winter.

An eastern chipmunk

The next time you walk by a hole, stop and think.

A striped skunk digs a hole.

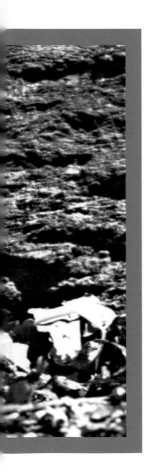

Who dug this hole?
Who might be living
down there?

How do we become fluent readers? We interpret, or decode, the written word. Knowledge of phonics—the rules and patterns for pronouncing letters—is essential. When we come upon a word we cannot figure out by any other strategy, we need to sound out that word.

Here are some very effective tools to help early readers along their way. Use the "add-on" technique to sound out unknown words. Simply add one sound at a time, always pronouncing previous sounds. For instance, to sound out the word **cat**, first say **c**, then **c-a**, then **c-a-t**, and finally the entire word **cat**. Reading "chunks" of letters is another important skill. These are patterns of two or more letters that make one sound.

Words from this book appear below. The markings are clues to help children master phonics rules and patterns. All consonant sounds are circled. Single vowels are either long –, short ˘, or silent /. Have fun with phonics, and a fluent reader will emerge.

Circle all double consonants, but remember to say the sound only one time when you sound out the word.

dĭgging   nĭbble

răbbĭt   wĭll

Circle all consonant clusters and blend them into one sound instead of two separate sounds.

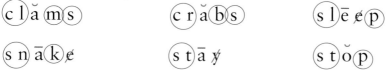

30

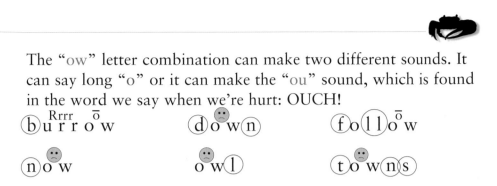

The "ow" letter combination can make two different sounds. It can say long "o" or it can make the "ou" sound, which is found in the word we say when we're hurt: OUCH!

ⓑu r r o w
ⓓo w ⓝ
ⓕo ⓛⓛo w
ⓝo w
o wⓛ
ⓣo w ⓝⓢ

The sound of the vowel combination "oi" is found in the word "oil."

ⓜo i ⓢ t
ⓢo iⓛ

fun facts

- Ants are very strong in relation to their size. They can carry ten to twenty times their body weight.
- Prairie dog towns can cover hundreds of acres of land. One town discovered in the nineteenth century was as big as Belgium.
- Woodpeckers don't get headaches from hammering because their heads are filled with pockets of air that cushion their head bones as they drill for food or bore their tunnels.
- Boring clams can drill through solid rock. It takes these clams eight years to complete the same task that an oil drill can perform in two minutes.
- European moles will sometimes heap up piles of soil weighing up to 1,650 lb (750 kg).

glossary/index

about the author

Anita Holmes is both a writer and an editor with a long career in children's and educational publishing. She has a special interest in nature, gardening, and the environment and has written numerous articles and award-winning books for children on these subjects. Ms. Holmes lives in Norfolk, Connecticut.

CRANBURY PUBLIC LIBRARY

3 9380 00047949 4

⑤

CRANBURY PUBLIC LIBRARY
23 North Main Street
Cranbury, NJ 08512

MAR 25 '03